ZIGMUND PALFFY

BILLY SMITH

PAT LaFONTAINE

BOB NYSTROM

DENIS POTVIN

ALEXAI YASHIN

PIERRE TURGEON

MIKE BOSSY

BOB BOURNE

MICHAEL PECA

JOHN TONELLI

BRYAN TROTTIER

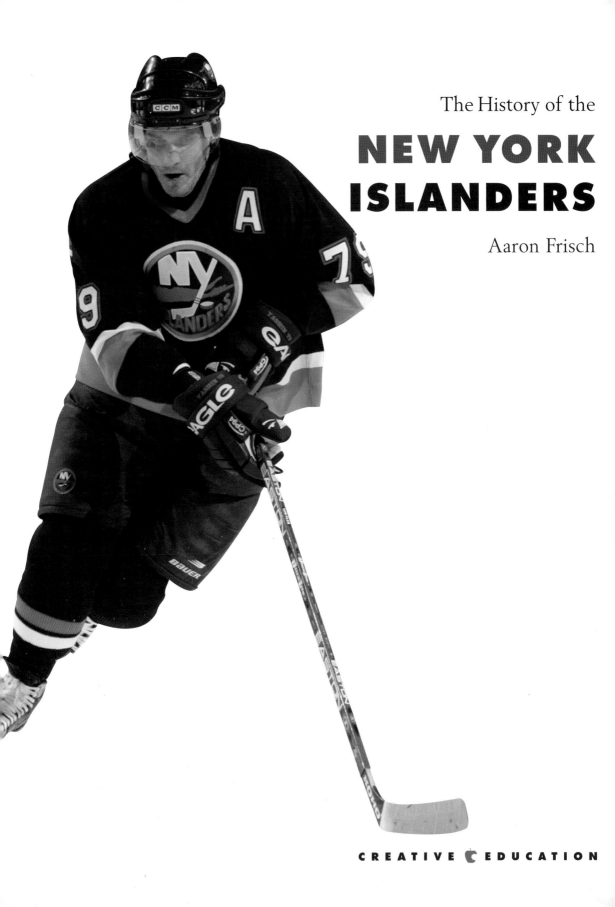

The History of the

NEW YORK
ISLANDERS

Aaron Frisch

CREATIVE ◖ EDUCATION

Published by Creative Education, 123 South Broad Street, Mankato, MN 56001

Creative Education is an imprint of The Creative Company.

Designed by Rita Marshall.

Photographs by Bruce Bennett Studios, Getty Images (Al Bello/NHLI, Ezra Shaw,

Rick Stewart/NHLI), Hockey Hall of Fame (London Life-Portnoy, Mecca), Icon Sports Media Inc.

(Robert Beck, Manny Millan), SportsChrome USA (Craig Melvin)

Library of Congress Cataloging-in-Publication Data

Frisch, Aaron. The history of the New York Islanders / by Aaron Frisch.

p. cm. — (Stanley Cup champions)   ISBN 1-58341-276-X

Summary: Presents the history, players, and accomplishments of the New York Islanders.

1. New York Islanders (Hockey team)—History—Juvenile literature.

[1. New York Islanders (Hockey team)—History. 2. Hockey—History.]

I. Title. II. Series (Mankato, Minn.).

GV848.N4 F75 2003   796.962'64'0974721—dc21   2002034933

First Edition 9 8 7 6 5 4 3 2 1

LONG ISLAND IS A MASS OF LAND THAT FORMS THE

SOUTHEASTERN PART OF THE STATE OF NEW YORK.

THE EASTERN SIDE OF THIS LONG, NARROW ISLAND

has many farms, fishing villages, and resorts along the Atlantic Ocean.

The western side features dense urban population, as two of the

island's four counties—Kings and Queens—are part of New York

City. Although it is only about 1,700 square miles in size, Long

Island has a population higher than most states in America.

In the late 1960s and early '70s, the National Hockey League

(NHL) underwent a period of rapid expansion. The league consid-

ered Long Island's large population—as well as New York's great love

for sports—and saw the region as the perfect place to add a fran-

chise. In 1972, a new team decked out in blue, orange, and white

took the ice. Naturally, that team was named the New York Islanders.

BILLY HARRIS

{A FRANCHISE IS BORN} The NHL was formed in 1917, and for many years it consisted of just six teams: the Boston Bruins,

In the biggest win of their inaugural season, the Islanders beat the mighty Bruins 9–7 in Boston.

Chicago Blackhawks, Detroit Red Wings, New York Rangers, Montreal Canadiens, and Toronto Maple Leafs. But in 1967—with hockey growing ever more popular as a spectator sport—the league began to expand at a quick pace, welcoming new franchises in cities throughout North America. By 1972, the NHL featured 16 teams, including the Islanders.

The Islanders were based in the Long Island city of Uniondale and played in the Nassau County Veterans Memorial Coliseum. The new team had its work cut out for it. New York was already home to the Rangers, who had just reached the 1972 Stanley Cup Finals and had a loyal fan base. The Islanders' challenge was to compete successfully with the Rangers for fan support.

GERRY HART

One of the
original
Islanders, goal-
tender Billy
Smith spent
17 seasons
with the club.

BILLY SMITH

"I knew it would be extremely difficult . . . ," said Bill Torrey, the Islanders' first general manager. "We would be sharing a market like no other team in the league, and sharing it with a dominant, powerful team. . . . I told the owners that we're not going to beat this team next door by taking the castoffs from other teams. We'd have to develop our own stars."

The Islanders began their building process by signing goaltender Billy Smith, defenseman Gerry Hart, and wing Ed Westfall from other NHL teams in the 1972 expansion draft. The club then drafted several talented youngsters, including center Lorne Henning and wings Billy Harris and Bob Nystrom. As expected, the Islanders took a beating their first season, setting a new NHL record by losing 60 games. The only good news was that there was nowhere to go from there but up.

ED WESTFALL

Defenseman Denis Potvin was as skilled at scoring as he was at delivering checks.

DENIS POTVIN

{ISLANDERS RISING} The Islanders made a number of key additions before their second season. First, they brought in new head coach Al Arbour. Then they added defensemen Dave Lewis and Bert Marshall. But no addition was more important than that of sensational rookie defenseman Denis Potvin.

New York selected Potvin with the first pick in the 1973 NHL Draft, and he wasted no time in becoming a star. His rugged good looks earned him lots of fan attention, and his play exceeded the highest expectations. He punished opponents with bone-jarring body checks, but he also amazed fans with his slick passing and deft shooting. With his help, the Islanders gave up 100 fewer goals than they had the year before. After the season, Potvin was awarded the Calder Trophy as the NHL's Rookie of the Year.

The Islanders took a big step forward in their third season.

The **1974–75** Islanders ended the season with 22 ties, setting a team record that still stands.

CLARK GILLIES

With the help of rookie wing Clark Gillies, New York leaped to a

33–25–22 record and made the playoffs. Then, in the playoffs, the

Islanders pulled off a major upset by toppling their crosstown rivals,

the Rangers. "The Rangers were 'The Team,'" Torrey later said. "For

us to win our first playoff series . . . against them as a tremendous

underdog had a lot to do with the success of our franchise."

But the Islanders weren't out of surprises yet. In the next round

of the playoffs, the Pittsburgh Penguins won the first three games of a

seven-game series. No team had come back from a 3–0

deficit to win a playoff series in 33 years. But the

upstart Islanders defied the odds, storming back to win

four straight games. They were beaten in the next

round by the defending Stanley Cup champion

Philadelphia Flyers, but Coach Arbour couldn't have been prouder of

his players. "If I called a practice next week," he said after the defeat,

"every one of them would show up."

{TROTTIER, BOSSY, AND A CUP} In 1976, a young center

named Bryan Trottier became the second Islanders player to win the

Calder Trophy. Trottier had an extraordinary sense of balance, which

allowed him to deliver crushing body checks or change direction in

a flash. He also seemed to have a knack for knowing where the

BRYAN TROTTIER

puck would be five seconds before it got there.

When the Islanders added talented wing Mike Bossy in 1977,

they were really on their way. In his first NHL press conference,

Bossy confidently predicted that he would "light the lamp" 50 times

his first year—a high goal indeed. The young winger was as good as

his word, setting a new NHL rookie record with 53 goals. He

remained a lethal scoring machine well into the 1980s, topping the prestigious 50-goal mark for nine straight seasons.

Behind Trottier, Bossy, and Potvin (who won the Norris Trophy as the NHL's best defenseman in 1976, 1978, and 1979), the Islanders enjoyed some fine seasons in the late '70s. Unfortunately, each of those seasons ended in a disappointing playoff loss. To make matters worse, the franchise teetered on the verge of collapse because of financial problems.

Things changed for the better in 1979–80, both financially and on the ice. After the franchise was purchased by new owners, the Islanders fought their way to the Stanley Cup Finals, where they beat the Philadelphia Flyers in three of the first five games. In game six, needing just one more win to claim the Stanley Cup, the Islanders took a 4–2 lead into the third period. But the hard-hitting

Explosive wing Mike Bossy led New York in goals every season from **1977–78** to **1986–87**.

MIKE BOSSY

Like the great
Denis Potvin,
Vladimir
Malakhov was
a tough and
talented
defender.

Flyers silenced Islanders fans by fighting back and netting two goals to force sudden-death overtime.

Bob Nystrom
began the
Islanders'
reign of domi-
nance with
his dramatic
goal in the
1980 finals.

The situation was now desperate for the Islanders. If they scored first, they would win the championship. If the Flyers scored first, the deciding game seven would take place at the Spectrum in Philadelphia, where the Flyers were nearly invincible. "You're just dying inside," Bill Torrey explained. "You're thinking about the first days, and the last two years in the playoffs, and . . . going back to Philadelphia if we lose."

Both teams played iron-clad defense early in the extra period. But at 7:11 of the overtime period, Islanders wing John Tonelli zipped a pass to fellow wing Bob Nystrom, who steered it past the Flyers goalie and into the net. The Nassau Coliseum crowd erupted in joy as the Islanders bench emptied onto the ice in a mad celebra-

BOB NYSTROM

tion. New York had its first Stanley Cup champion in 40 years.

{A DYNASTY . . . AND DECLINE} The Islanders' 1980 championship was the start of one of the greatest dynasties in NHL his-

tory. From 1979–80 to 1982–83, the Islanders averaged 45 wins per

season and captured four straight Stanley Cups. In 1981, New York

lost only three games in four playoff rounds and beat the Minnesota

North Stars for the Cup. In 1982, the Islanders swept the Vancouver

Canucks in the finals, and in 1983, they swept the Edmonton Oilers

to complete their amazing "four-peat."

There was no secret to the Islanders' dominance.

The club was loaded with talented players committed

to teamwork. The high-scoring Bossy (68 goals in

1980–81) and versatile Trottier (79 assists in 1981–82)

deserved much of the credit, but the Islanders also featured such

stars as goalie Billy Smith, center Bob Bourne, wing John Tonelli,

and, of course, Denis Potvin. These players were the heart of a

squad that *New York Times* writer George Vescey called "the best

sports team of this generation."

At the end of the 1983–84 season, New York came up short in

its bid for a fifth straight Stanley Cup, losing to the Oilers and star

center Wayne Gretzky in the finals. A year later, the Islanders were

JOHN TONELLI

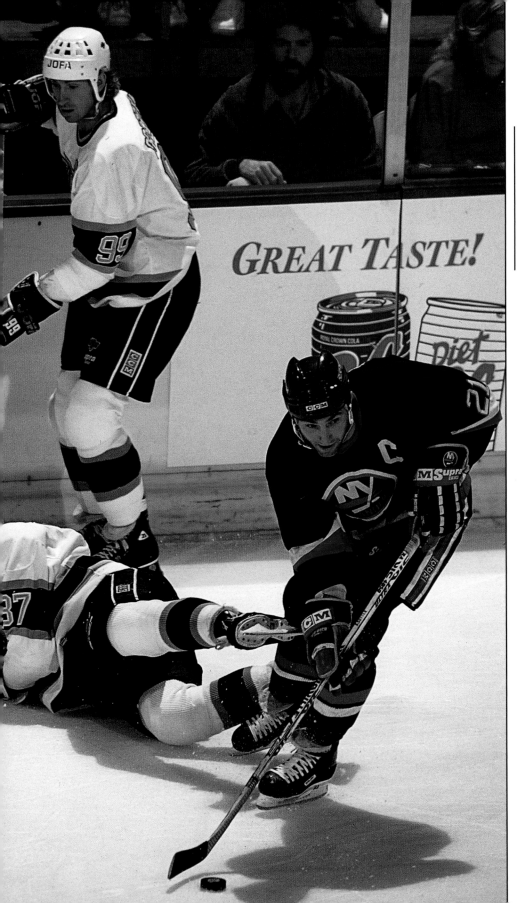

GREAT TASTE!

A star of the **'80s**, center Brent Sutter wore the blue and orange for 12 seasons.

BRENT SUTTER

thumped by the Flyers in the Patrick Division Finals. "Nobody stays on top forever," Torrey said. "Sooner or later you're going to lose. The question is how long will it take to get back."

After falling from the top, the Islanders looked to rebound behind such young stars as centers Brent Sutter and Pat LaFontaine. The fiery Sutter was a terrific all-around player, but LaFontaine was even

Pierre Turgeon succeeded Mike Bossy and Pat LaFontaine as the Islanders' go-to scorer.

better. Arriving in 1983, he quickly became a fan favorite thanks to his speed, agility, brilliant stickwork, and good looks. Yet despite this talent, the Islanders declined in the late 1980s, making an early playoff exit every year.

{THE NOT-SO-NOTABLE '90s} The 1990s started poorly for the Islanders. The franchise was again plagued by financial problems, and in 1992, new team owners ended Bill Torrey's 20-year reign as general manager. On top of that, LaFontaine—wanting a

PIERRE TURGEON

bigger and richer contract—asked to be traded and was sent to the

Buffalo Sabres.

Islanders fans were sad to see LaFontaine go, but the trade

brought a new star to New York: soft-spoken center Pierre Turgeon.

Although a graceful skater and superb puck-handler, Turgeon had

never quite reached the potential expected of him in Buffalo. The move to Long Island seemed to inspire him, however. In 1992–93,

he delighted the New York faithful by netting 58 goals and racking

up 132 points (goals plus assists).

Behind Turgeon's superb season, the Islanders

leaped to a 40–37–7 record in 1992–93. Center

Ray Ferraro and wing Derek King added offensive

firepower, and Soviet standouts Vladimir Malakhov

Rugged enforcer Darius Kasparaitis anchored New York's defensive unit for five seasons.

and Darius Kasparaitis spearheaded a tough defense as the Islanders

rolled into the playoffs. There they stunned the two-time defending

Stanley Cup champion Pittsburgh Penguins before losing to the

Montreal Canadiens. "This is only the beginning of something good

for this team and this franchise," predicted Al Arbour.

Unfortunately, that prediction was off the mark. The Islanders

faded to 36–36–12 the next season and were quickly beaten in the

playoffs. After the loss, Arbour stepped down as the team's leader

D. KASPARAITIS

after coaching in an NHL-record 1,601 games. That was the last respectable season the team would put together for a while.

Hard-shooting winger Zigmund Palffy scored hat tricks in back-to-back games in March **1996**.

{A SLUMP—AND SURGE} In 1995, former NHL defenseman Mike Milbury was named the Islanders' new general manager. Milbury spent the next seven seasons wheeling and dealing in an effort to build a winner. During those years, the team passed under the control of five ownership groups and eight coaches. Nothing worked. Fans stopped coming to Nassau Coliseum as the Islanders hit rock bottom, averaging fewer than 24 wins a season and missing the playoffs every year.

Still, the Islanders featured some excellent players during the late 1990s. Among them were Ferraro, defensemen Rich Pilon and Kenny Jonsson, and wings Zigmund Palffy and Mariusz Czerkawski. The brightest of these standouts was Palffy, one of the NHL's best

ZIGMUND PALFFY

shooters. The young wing left opposing goalies bewildered with his slick passing and accurate slap shots, averaging 45 goals a season from 1995–96 to 1997–98. Sadly, after becoming embroiled in a contract dispute in 1999, Palffy was traded away.

Mariusz Czerkawski had his best season yet in **2000–01**, leading the Islanders with 62 points.

The team's fortunes finally began to turn in 2000, when Charles Wang and Sanjay Kumar—two computer company executives—purchased the Islanders. The new owners were committed to winning and quickly expanded the club's payroll, enabling New York to sign talented wing Mark Parrish and defenseman Roman Hamrlik.

The Islanders missed the playoffs again in 2001, but they scored big in the off-season. The club signed veteran goalie Chris Osgood, who had previously helped Detroit win two Stanley Cups. In two huge trades, the team also added elite centers Alexai Yashin

M. CZERKAWSKI

Hustling wing Mark Parrish was expected to help New York rise in the standings.

MARK PARRISH

A key team leader, Alexai Yashin boasted a rare combination of skill and strength.

ALEXAI YASHIN

and Michael Peca. Yashin was a 6-foot-3 and 225-pound bruiser with a terrific slap shot, and the small but fierce Peca was a natural leader.

Fans hoped that wing Mattias Weinhandl would boost the offense in **2003–04** and beyond.

Led by these new stars, the Islanders won 42 games in 2001–02 and ended their playoff drought. Even though they were edged out of the first round of the playoffs by the Toronto Maple Leafs, the Islanders were on the rise once again. "Our expectations for ourselves are higher than anyone else's," said Parrish. "Our goal is to be a powerhouse and to make a run at the Stanley Cup."

The New York Islanders have packed a lot of excitement into a history that spans barely 30 years. The franchise boasts four Stanley Cups and a list of former and current greats that includes such names as Potvin, Trottier, Bossy, LaFontaine, and Peca. As this proud team fights its way up the standings, it likely won't be long before that big silver cup returns to the island.

M. WEINHANDL